SILVERTONE

BOOKS BY DZVINIA ORLOWSKY

A Handful of Bees
Edge of House
Except for One Obscene Brushstroke
Convertible Night, Flurry of Stones
Silvertone

SILVERTONE

DZVINIA ORLOWSKY

Dzvinia Orlowsky (signature)

CARNEGIE MELLON UNIVERSITY PRESS
PITTSBURGH 2013

Acknowledgments

Grateful acknowledgment is made to the publications in which some of these poems first appeared, sometimes in different form:

10 x 3 Plus: "Still As I Was"; *Alembic*: "North of Patsy Cline," "Stung," "Stolen," "Black Dog"; *Bitter Oleander*: "Wild Violets"; *Cardinal Points*: "What I Inherited," "Foreign Woman"; *Connotations*: "Muse," "Advent Calendar," "To See a Horse"; *The Drunken Boat*: "The Fox," "Shoe Laces," "Uncle," "The Grass Tall Enough," "Borscht"; *Great River Review*: "Illegible Postcards"; *The Green Mountains Review*: "In God's Language," "Prolonged," "My Acupuncturist Discovers a Point," "Early Hour," "Jesus Loves Fat People"; *Laurel Review*: "How to Memorize Music," "At the Waist"; *The Minnesota Review*: "Used Boat," "Praying to Fra Lippi's Mistress"; *Oscillation*: "Roses in Their Hands"; *Ploughshares*: "Size Zero"; *Plume*: "Firing My Father's Mossberg"; *Salt Hill*: "Baptism"; *Solstice Literary Magazine*: "Silvertone," "Her Gift," "Smoke on the Water"

I would like to thank Franz Wright, Nancy Mitchell, Jeff Friedman, and Melanie Drane for many years of friendship and the gift of their words. Thank you, Nancy, in particular, for your caring, generous insight and help on these and other poems. Many thanks also to the following individuals and communities for years of friendship and support: Alan Britt, Alex Motyl, Kathi Aguero, Ira Sadoff, Catherine Sasanov, Gary Duehr, Lee Hope, Gloria Mindock, Mike Steinberg, Jack Driscoll, Barbara Carlson, Meg Kearney, Tanya Whiton and all Solstice Writers, Pine Manor College, Keene State College, and Cornelia Street Café. My deepest gratitude to you, Cynthia Lamb, for all your help and support, and especially to Gerald Costanzo, *thank you*, for your belief in my work throughout the years.

Book design: Veronica Kawka

Contents

for Jay, Max and Raisa
with love, always

&

for Nancy Mitchell
with love, always, too

I

"You never get finished with this subject, your mother and your father."

—Robert Lowell

"I'll play it first then tell you what it is later."

—Miles Davis

SMOKE ON THE WATER

In China, the fans no longer give
a damn about Deep Purple's Last World
Tour, but our town's Middle School band
conductress still showcases the song,
pushing the tempo fast, baton raised,
under arms swinging fiercely
like hammocks
in a Midwest storm.

Once, cheerleader-sexy under bleachers
in cold November air,
the pride of our county
is now a dry-cleaner's
hot ticket sweating profusely
in a starched three-quarter-sleeved
white jacket.

The horn section seems to suffer
most—black slacks, starched shirts
wafting Axe—hair water-slicked,
ears and cheeks flaming red,
eyes burning through sheet music,
every note blown cavernous
into just *some adult shit song.*

Disperse the smoke,
Drain the water.

Long stripped of Purple's
leather pants and sooty asses,
parents love her song choice.
It signals the end of the school year,
dented rental instruments turned in,
locked all summer in their metal cages.

As long as they start and end together,
doesn't matter what they play in between.

My husband's own favorite:
Any one hurt?

We fold our programs, let out a collective
discreet sigh of relief, smile as we file
to our cars, a light drumming of rain
on the hood—

Did we really think we'd ever lose
those heavy booted chords?

No turning back
the worn tape rattles
the car's speakers' bass blast,
windshield wipers slashing
the short ride home.

BLACK DOG
Solstice Summer Writers' Conference, 2006

It's a lie we go on forever
if we love a favorite song or poem deeply enough.

But tonight under the college president's dining room's
best-bet dimmed lights,
ice coolers are packed with beers,
and outside, a sudden summer thunderstorm
has just missed the campus.

My 14-year-old son, drafted as the night's DJ,
doesn't know what writers want to hear.
He wants to make sure he gets it right:

Paperback Writer, Respect . . . ?

He flags me over, about to select a song
he's seen me let go of the steering wheel for,
shimmying my shoulders,
clicking my fingers,
air conditioner cranked,
feeling deliciously dangerous
mouthing lyrics to strangers
staring as they pass.

For him, I'll make sure
whatever he chooses appears to be
an immediate hit,
not care who's looking
across the empty dance floor
as I throw myself in wild abandon
into its center,
hoping for one willing partner.

But I have worried for nothing.
When Max switches to Led Zeppelin's "Black Dog,"
Trooper, the director's three-legged Lab,

cameo, mascot, limps excitedly onto the dance floor
as if on cue.

It's a lie we go on forever
even if we love a favorite song or poem deeply enough.
And I have loved this song for a long time.
But tonight, it's mascot's.

Judging by the way his whole back wags,
swinging its weight, risking his balance
on the polished floor,
he can barely contain himself
that we have come.

USED BOAT

If it starts, the engine alone is worth
the asking price, not to mention the trailer hitch—
clearly a giveaway. Someone could make
a fortune restoring this classic,
with new slipcovers return its luster,
dead moths and acorns swept free,
the mouse's nest dislodged
from a torn life vest.

A car slows down only to speed up again
as the driver and his wife or girlfriend
see my husband start to walk toward them,
a cracked plastic rake in his hand.

Looking at our boat, I wonder if there's
anything that screams as loud:
it devours gas;
our backs can't take the open waves anymore;
the freezer stayed
empty of fish all summer;
Even with sunblock,
my face will soon
resemble my elbow.

But like a heavy iron
docked on an ironing board,
it fills the yard
with promise,
waits for the smooth deal that will hitch
itself onto a young family's Ford truck.

And they come—mom, dad, son,
together, to decide.
They hand us
five hundred dollar bills.

It's our job to add the mild look of envy
to their happy decision. A look that says,
if we had the money, we would
buy it from ourselves.

The mermaid on the ripped cushion
seductively curling her heavy tail,
whose wink was never for us,
we eagerly throw in for free.

SILVERTONE

1.

Every Friday my father's voice, drunk
on plum Slivovitz, rose from our basement
through the heating vent on my bedroom floor,
not a light-hearted warble—a deeper velvet
vibrato, the color of his eyes.

Alternating three minor chords,
he'd strum his guitar, lips pursed,
angelic as an adult Hummel figurine,
hold each note until each word released
from the luscious center, stretched
like taffy into a *Boulevard of Broken Dreams*
or *Once-upon-a-time-there-was-a-tavern.*

Across from him, my mother, shoulders back—
black turtlenecked, black stockinged, legs
crossed and wrapped around a barstool,
poured herself another half glass
of Schwarze Katz wine,
the small insignia plastic black cat
dangling from the bottle's neck.
She'd lean toward him, cautiously,
as if he were a wren that could
be easily frightened away.

She'd plead—*please play
the sad song again*—the one
about the village girl who, ignoring her mother's warning,
slipped into night to meet her moody lover,
but not before first inspecting
her reflection in the family's well.
Pushing her hair away from her face
to check the curve of her cheek,
she leaned over too far, fell in,

but no one heard her cries,
no one wept in chorus.

2.

Once I was caught spying on them—
envying their adult fun earned crossing
the ocean from Kiev to New York,
then down long back roads to Ohio.
I was supposed to be asleep
and out of their way.
But I wanted to hear my father's voice,
see my mother fall in love with him again
as he carefully plucked the strings
that now look rusted, tainted,

medieval—as if they could slice
through thick bread or a hard wheel of cheese,
or could send an arrow flying.
They could cut fingers, too,
if the player didn't know how to press them
properly, fingertips angled just right,
nails evenly trimmed.

I was sent immediately to bed. No second
goodnight, no quick cup of water.

3.

In the Scituate Music Shop,
a young guitarist-salesman holds Father's guitar up
to the window. He says the neck is warped.
The strings are shot from human sweat—
not enough alcohol rubbed on them over the years.
I could replace the strings,
but they'd barely sound against the badly damaged frets.
He turns it upside down and shakes it
until my father's Lucite pick
falls out like a tooth.

Silvertone: Sears and Roebuck, he mumbles. Catalog ordered
in the '50s. There were a lot of them back then.

It was not the guitar I imagined my father bartered
from gypsies and carried through harsh winters
with barely a shield to protect it,
the one he and my mother made love next to
for the first time, the guitar
propped on the bed next to them,
the large tear-shaped guard
and wooden bridges
I thought I was born of.

Instead, it's 1959. My father sits near their bedroom window,
his black glasses perched at the end of his nose:
Doc Orlowsky of Brunswick
prudently studying each guitar,
imagining the weight of its wooden body
in his lap,
his left hand circled around the neck,
fingers poised, right arm resting heavily.

He decides on the one pictured slung over
the shoulder of a Midwest cowboy,
the guitar sturdy enough to take,
if need be, to a fallout shelter.

4.

The salesman continues to tilt the guitar
in every direction, shake it violently,
upside down, like an obstetrician, as if to make it cry
or to force whatever was still wedged or stubborn
out of the sound hole:

my mother's shiny bobby pins loosened
from her hair—no, further:
Mother, herself, hanging
onto her wine glass,

Father reaching deep,
fingers stretched into a seventh chord,
to find his soul—
fur hat,
cowboy hat,
a bird.

Not bad, he says,
for what they were.

He twists the tuning pins with pliers
to see if, one last time, they might budge
then, resigned, lifts my father's Silvertone over the glass
counter case. Handing it over to me,
it's now as weightless as a stingy bouquet of carnations
presented at the end of a paltry recital.
Good luck, he says.
It's so light I can barely carry it.

Roses in Their Hands

White Roses

A note card with hand-painted white roses says *devastated not to attend a funeral*, which will never take place. No one could believe that this was her last wish: simply to be blessed by a handsome, thick-bearded priest, all things clamoring forgiven, then cremated with her personal letters, her stack of black and white photographs my father took of her leaning slightly forward as she opens the door of a shrine-sized refrigerator wearing only a baby doll nightie, her nipples cold and erect in the diffuse, almost holy light.

Red Roses

Why wouldn't she want to pose in a baby doll nightie while her breasts were still firm and her hips, curved like the contours of my father's guitar? She already knew she had dark, seductive eyes—eyes a young girl might readily be punished for having, eyes that peeked quickly over a book taking in the lightly falling snow riding the tram on the way to school, eyes that unnerved the Russian geography teacher who accused her of deliberately darkening her lashes with coal dust. He made her rub and re-rub her eyes with his rough white handkerchief, then wrote *liar* in her notebook because the eyes he hoped would smear into dangerous and dusky thunder clouds converging over a nocturnal river only turned red.

Green Roses

My father too, the doctor, of whom it might be assumed his medical career was most important to him, who would believe he harbored the soul of a musician, a lyric poet who could feel the green from grass rising up through his bare feet? He wanted most to feel my mother's eyes watching him as his fingers moved freely over the guitar neck pressing and releasing the strings over the frets; the other hand, openly strumming; and she, to stay forever in full bloom, half naked, just about to prepare a snack out of air and a low-watt bulb, opening the refrigerator door.

II

BAPTISM

Lightly scented oil trickled
off my forehead and into the font,
lay like a skin on the water.
For a second, I may have thought

I was asked to drown—though no life yet
to flash before my eyes—just birth,
a green room filled with applause.
After that, one unremitting nap,

both hands tucked in tiny socks,
my soft nails growing too fast.
Squinting to see who'd startled
me awake, I was calmed back to my

Godmother's bottomless rocking.
I surrendered, wrinkled, red-faced,
some later said *ugly as a baby hyena*,
a few spiked threads of hair

the color of beeswax.
My mother clutched a candle
as though it were a bowed and twisted
rose scraped of its thorns.

Handpicked choir voices rolled forward
crashing over the tops of pews.
Where could I run, days heavy,
in my mother-of-pearl baby shoes?

On the 16 mm film, stained glass appeared gray.
Everyone gathered to see me made pure,
to keep me from being numbered
among the beasts.

In God's Language

Each liturgical word
hung like a sun out on a branch.

Each was ours to behold—
a promise of resurrection

while the earth slowly turned
into a large cemetery.

We learned to know the difference:

Words from hell sounded like crackling fire,
syllables spitting through droughts of empty pews.

Words from heaven sounded like ringing glass
through which we rose,

our bodies, soprano,
the crucifix, a musical notation.

ADVENT CALENDAR

1.

It doesn't matter how you're dressed.
Open that first door.

There it is—a candy cane.
Sorry.

You expected something better?
Sacred as a star

calling back to you.

2.

Open the next day's door—

a startled squirrel clutching a nut
like a grenade.

3.

Try another—

a one-winged
wind-saturated dinner goose

to keep you curious
and hungry in this life.

4.

Savor each easy-

pull gold tassel,
open the next-to-last door.

Voilà:
Black velvet-clad party children,
a nutcracker's open mouth

empty as a yard sale
play set kitchen shelf.

5.

The last door, admit it,
you also rushed ahead to open,

before someone lit a candle
and called the door a clock,

or a window,
a mirror—

There, peeking out of straw,
a large piece of chocolate.

You thought you heard
a donkey bray,

and prayed for the wise men to come.

PRAYING TO FRA LIPPI'S MISTRESS

Make them forget there's such a thing as flesh.
—Robert Browning

1.

Opening the triptych panels wide, I kissed faceless

what I thought
for years was the true Madonna

saying prayers before I pulled back my bedding,
washed off my make-up.

I watched her disappear over time,
smear into a red window.

2.

In art history books we learned she wasn't sacred after all,

but, rather, Friar Lippi's mistress,
Lucrezia Buti,

for whom he risked everything—

set against steep cliffs
and stunted trees,

the glow of her skin
rising over the banks of angels.

3.

I've watched my daughter press her cheek
against the icon,

slowly trace with her finger
the large pear-shaped pearl

hung low on the Madonna's shaved,
perfectly domed forehead.

But if the Madonna wasn't sacred to Fra Lippi, what
would he have done with us?

Would he have painted the skin
of my daughter's cheek

as she knelt in prayer, her long brown hair
cascading down her back?

She places a kiss
on what's left of Lucrezia's face.

Afterwards, she gently wipes her mark.

4.

There's space left by adoration
to place one's face.

This is a woman, this is flesh.
We know what's ours to pray for—

all of us, sumptuous vanishing points.

Cloud of breath,
heavy dew.

The Grass Tall Enough

1.

The bust of Taras Schevchenko, national poet,
stood erect in a field,

determined as stone.
We would march to him, honor him,

cut back the weeds.
For this our parents waved goodbye to us

for three weeks of camp every summer.
The Homeland they'd remind us

before driving away.
For this, they saved.

2.

The Amish
driving their carriages

on a dirt Middlefield road
turned their heads

to face what had just passed—
a line of uniformed children, single file

and brown ankle-socked,
the synchronized clock work of our feet.

3.

Yet, standing before his heroic head,
we wondered of what use were our meager offerings,

chosen token sacrifices
placed obediently on the ground:

snapped gum wrapper chains,
tabs pulled from pilfered soda cans,

the grass tall enough for lies.

A Polaroid of my beloved pound-found
mutt, Vasha,

her eyes averted,
paw raised—

I hesitated to leave behind.

Finely lined pockets
turned inside out,

how quickly a hand
turns up empty.

Shoe Laces

I was always slow to tie the adult-size sneaker
nailed to a small wooden board
made for practicing on,
one lace crossed over the other,
then *quick-dip-under*, my hands
coming up empty and questioning
like those of a magician's whose
signature trick has just gone sour,
the failproof knot dropped.

BORSCHT

Each Epiphany, clear blood
sipped off polished silver spoons,
no slivers of beets to tempt us into biting,
we longed to curl our tongues
around the "little ears"—*Yshka*,
folded boiled dough stuffed
with fried onions and mushrooms
and pinched closed—
or Chinese dumplings to the Stop & Shop clerk—
three per guest crowding each small ceramic bowl.

But as children we feared they could hear
our thoughts:
Johnny masturbated.
Diane touched the classroom's *Do not touch!*
clay model volcano!—
her finger destined to blaze
like a Pascal candle.

After company left, Mother poured the holy
soup down the drain.
We were safe
once again
to believe
the soup's steam
whispered only its flavors.

UNCLE

Bits of mustard ham stained the linen napkin,
dropped off his moustache
as he'd first chew then whisper,
Do you want to see me roll my tongue
into a fat cigar? Sure, my sister would answer
resigned, kicking me under the table.
Then after dinner, standing
too close to us at the sink,
he'd offer up his middle finger:
I can make a baby with just this!
He'd wait for us to laugh.
In the next room, Mother snapped a napkin
to get our attention. She tapped her fingertip
against her right earlobe:
He's hard of hearing—

Were he alive now, he'd never pass through airport security,
his overcoat pockets stuffed
with gifts: Manitoba souvenir fork spoons,
lacquered *matryoshkas,*
two stuffed, plush velvet mushrooms
we called *what-the-hells,*
their *X* eyes and long grins
stitched with gold thread.

Muggy Sunday afternoons,
refreshed after a second shower,
smelling of cologne,
his face flushed with color,
fingernails surgeon-scrubbed,
he'd stare at us long and hard,
tap his middle finger against
the hot tea glass making sure we noticed, too,
his silver cufflinks.
Only Mother laughed,
offering more tea.

After all, he was family.
And he'd traveled so far.

STOLEN

1.

Pretending to be looking for Band-Aids,
we pulled them from the back of the drawer
gauzy teddies, zebra-striped *baby doll nighties* we held

up to the window light, thinking they were missing curtains
slipping freely through our hands
until we could see that we could try them on,

undressed to the waist, each sister exposed
through the transparent cloth. Our breasts were
too small for the under-wired, lace push-up bras

arranged into rows behind the flannels.
We rolled them up and pushed them back.
What else did Mother hide in the heaviest drawer?

Thick shot glasses, joke shop rubber vomit,
a siren purple wig—
Did this make Father laugh, his gold molar

glinting in the dark, before he passed away,
before our mother had his crown pierced,
affixed onto her glittering charm bracelet?

2.

But who took the odd small, rock sculpture
stacked like a bear, *love* written
where its belly button might've been

lifting it off the bamboo shelf in the guest room,
the ceramic Model T Ford evergreen
plant holder from the kitchen windowsill,

a poster of a topless woman bending
forward, a watering can in her hand,
from behind the washing machine—they all

appeared and equally quickly disappeared.

3.

Or did we take them in our sleep,
our mother lighting the way with a candle?
Their gone missing was enough to punish us,

send us straight into hell, blistering
and teeming, the devils angry and red
as her holiday lipstick.

4.

In daylight, we rushed out into the wind, tossed
our cloth dolls high over telephone wires,
waiting to see if they'd catch or fall,

then stand them up on wobbly legs.
Sometimes we made them
faint in beautiful positions, hand to brow.

Other times, feeling cruel, we punched them,
knowing God, watching, might steal us as ransom
from *Pearl Road* where we lived

and return us old, too late, our hair
graying, bones too slight to carry
a water pail to our horse in the meadow—

He, too, one day disappeared, neglected,
his eyes rimmed with green-eyed flies
though there were days we swore we saw him

like a mirage in the rising heat
grazing peacefully just past the neighbor's
heavy, lidded gladiolas.

III

WHAT I INHERITED

Lipstick

It was the shock of pre-party red to her lips that my sister and
I stared long into—its fleshy open bull's-eye, hungry Venus
Flytrap, outlined with dark borders, an accent mole as if her
face were a clock painted by Magritte, a perfect dot right about
at 4:00. It was never *Mum* or *Mother* we saw coming down the
hall or standing in half-light by her bedroom door. It was her red
lipstick. She kissed the rim of her Gimlet glass. She kissed the
back of her hand. She kissed squares of toilet paper. She must
have kissed us too though upon waking, studying our faces in the
mirror, checking our palms, we never found proof.

A Need to Keep Moving

Train leaving! my father calls out as my sister and I, squeamish,
careful not to touch each other's bare feet, pile on our parents'
bed. It's our way of rehearsing for, or altogether avoiding disas-
ter—all of us together, first days then years, throwing salt over
our shoulders, spitting quickly to the side when passing a grave-
yard, stepping twice over a threshold, or tossing spare change
onto the floor of a brand new car.

He presses his index finger lightly against his lips, closes his eyes.
German bombs whistle heavy-bellied from the sky. One explodes
next to our swaybacked horse at the edge of his barbedwired
pasture, another one blows up our four-foot above-ground swim-
ming pool sending fragments of inflatable rafts, flippers, goggles,
spinning into the sky. We feel safe knowing we are accounted for
before a third bomb blasts out of the otherwise soundless night
shattering unmade beds, fracturing mirrors, scattering neighbor-
ing families in human litters of fire.

Tracking Names Easily Forgotten

For now their names stay with me: *Figa, Vasha, Matska, Bobuk,
Horoshok*—mostly mutts from accidental litters. Some could do
tricks—climb a tree after a cat, lap beer out of a mug; but all,

particularly the pure breeds, were destined for misfortune. *Fifi,* an overweight standard dachshund, couldn't digest a mouse after killing and swallowing it. *Aza,* our Chihuahua, one winter day mysteriously rolled out of her baby blanket, out the unlocked front door and under the wheel of the first speeding car. While my mother stood in the middle of the road screaming *Murderers!,* I hid in the bathroom covering my ears with my hands. Tall summer grass rippling with an approaching storm took the last dog, *Masha,* collarless and meadow-wild.

Buried Bell

The Sohio station attendant, *Mike,* stitched in red above the pocket of his blue uniform, leaned into the window of the backseat where I sat, *Cindy and Sue,* my paper dolls, lined up on the seat.

Shaking his head he asked my parents in the front seat, *Pelagia Dzvinia? Now what kind of name is that for a little girl?*

My mother whispered under her breath: *Dzvinia, Dzvinka, Dzvenyslava. Wild flower. A Little Bell. Noble one. Pelagia, Pelahia. Martyr. Daughter of the sea.*

Handing my father the receipt Mike said, *Let me give you a little advice . . . keep it simple . . . friendly, American.* He looked back at me appraisingly, and after a few seconds he nodded his head saying, *She looks like a Peggy . . . yea, Peggy.*

Just in time for first grade, my father agreed, his eyes beaming at me from the rearview mirror, as he pulled out of the station. Through the back window I watched the attendant grow smaller and smaller, my father's view of the highway ahead framed by the windshield, every smudge swiped and drying clean.

FOREIGN WOMAN

She rarely visited her young grandchildren.
But when she did and they misbehaved
by crying or pulling on the dog's tail,
she'd lean forward, point her finger,
warn *Baba never coming again.*

Then she'd pass the chipped plate
of all she had to offer:
a Salvation Army-purchased
foldout playpen with exposed rusted
screws, the wooden duck placed inside
with torn rubber flapper feet
and a lead paint nose,
the oversized stuffed burlap Teddy Bear
for a pillow,
the naked doll left out in the rain, in the sun
with missing tufts of hair,
a cloud of gnats circling her pink torso.
She named her *Va-va,* foreign woman.

If she ever held them, I didn't see it;
if she ever held me, I don't remember.
Now holding in my hand
what she kept
like medicine near her bed,
a single bruised apple,
its ripe *never.*

FIRING MY FATHER'S MOSSBERG

1.

At the shooting range,
my elbow raised, safety
unlocked, squeezing the trigger
I block out surrounding shots, whisper *breathe*

as if to my father,

a rebuttal to my husband's
You're scared of these things . . .

Scarlet leaves of sumac ambush
the periphery of an otherwise cleared path
over which the bullet could be fired.

2.

It was a loaded lie: the buck
hanging from our backyard tree
just sleeping in a frozen body,

its wide open eye, a mirror,
in which my hair split
and tied high into two pig-
tails brushed the fur
collar of my short down jacket,
curled into blond parenthesis
around my face.

3.

Father kept his Mossberg's
little brother, BB, hidden
behind sample prescription drugs
crammed and forgotten
in the bedroom oak cabinet.

He kept it to protect us
from the Hell's Angels
who revved their motorcycles,
swarmed like bees
onto a rotting pear,
circling the parking lot
of the restaurant next door.

Windows rattled, my bedroom
stained glass hexagons
of roses fell, broke on the floor.

4.

Father liked to point out
the tiny hole in the BB's slide—
in case it was ever stolen.

It had the capability, he said, to shoot
the shooter with the spent casing.

It had sense of humor, he said,
for a gun.

5.

Aluminum pie pans spin wildly
from branches of our cherry tree.

Crows flap their wings
shitting in terror.

We couldn't eat the cherries fast enough.
They softened on a plate,
exposed rancid gaping wounds,

black oozing bruises our tongues
learned quickly to avoid.

6.

Each time the target sheets
shudder then sway
loosely on the pulleys.

Distant pinpricks of December light
move and stay—

scattered bits of black feather
and sumac berries in winter . . .

And spirited from sleep, the astounded soul
Hangs for a moment bodiless and simple

. . . not exactly angels or simple

or the buck reawakened.

ILLEGIBLE POSTCARDS

Bone where we once misread *stone,*
fear rather than *dear.*

They dragged our neighbor outside,
not *We met our new neighbor, shared bread.*

Turn the card over to a golden field,
grain stalks clearly scripted against the sky.

My family gathers around our own warmed loaf.
A single white candle pierces the middle,

drips long wax lace onto the small wheat hill.
Was that tiny ink blot *not,* before *shot*—

Grandmother's feather-shaped eyes
sweeping through foreign woods

for her missing son? Dreams flowed loose,
tore on brambly banks.

In my father's handwriting, words spatter
rain steadily kicked us

on the back of a hand-painted
postcard where a skinny,

knock-kneed boy
clutches a wind-thrashed umbrella

in one hand, tilts to the weight
of a water pail in the other.

Fleeing, was this all
my mother and father had time to write

or standing here
all we could bear to read?:

*We were carried.
This morning*

*among flowers
we were married.*

WILD VIOLETS
—for Miroslaus & Tamara Orlowsky

They shadow earth that bears them,
single-letter alphabet of April's fields,

deep bottle blue of temples'
veins, eyes opened and closed

at like hours, lids half-
swollen above thawing ground.

Velvet assassins,
let me pluck them from Father's cold,

knit fingers where Mother lay a bouquet of them,
sift her ashes, twenty-nine years later,

for their bruised flecks.
They cannot grow under stone.

HER GIFT

Mother promised her gift to my sister and me was no matter if
we wanted her to or not, right after she'd die, she'd hurry back as
a steaming bowl of split pea soup or a glass flute of champagne
toasting her name day or any occasion that called for bare-legs
dancing in bright purple half-slips or running barefoot through
snow, screaming as we touch-tagged the nearest tree then turned
to run inside the wood-heated house, each log sputtering in
sluggish code. She promised to find *some way* to tell us what it
was really like to die, but in the meantime, we'd have to learn to
endure loneliness and long dark halls until a crow cawed or the
wooden banister knocked back.

For two nights my sister and I whispered *Mamo, mu z toboyu—
Mother, we're here with you,* into two long nights, finger-stroked
her hair away from the fevered aged child face, took turns
pressing our foreheads against hers, skin of our skin, listened as
through a glass held to a wall.

The morning she died we arrived to find a waxy vinyl curtain
encircling her bed protecting her from strangers' eyes, airborne
germs, the stifling August air we leaned into to take in *at peace—*
eyes closed, her mouth unlocked, sprung open like a large locket.

Did she cross the ash bridge to my father beaming as a newly-
wed, meeting her again after twenty-nine years, aged as she or
the same as the day he died? Did he remember to bring an empty
hard-shelled suitcase, the brass-trimmed traveling alarm, her
favorite white satin autograph dachshund—for years unsigned?
Was Grandmother there at the window, unseen to the rest of us,
sifting through morning light, dressed in her floor-dusted apron
around her thick waist, the last word in the argument she and
Mother started fifty years ago on her lips?

There were no secret notes for us inscribed in her skin, in the
tiny blue veins of her eyelids, or scripted in her gray-tipped hair
flared across the pillow. It looked as if she simply stopped wher-
ever she was, whatever she was thinking or doing, wherever she

thought she could still walk to if held up by her arms. She simply stopped, her face turned slightly to the right as if she were listening to something distant. In her hands she clutched a soft leather pouch—*God,* she would have said.

IV

JESUS LOVES FAT PEOPLE
Scrawled in pencil on an 8ᵗʰ grade
algebra book above a hand-drawn crucifix

The cross so deliberately and thickly drawn,
it could've been pulled off the wall
of some rustic pagan-Roman Catholic Church
leaving one of the stations unoccupied
and suffer-free. Tonight my young

daughter pushes her food away.
Everything is either a vein or fat or a strand
of hair clinging like a slack tourniquet.
It wasn't that long ago that I weighed
myself, my body disappeared,

the softness my husband couldn't find
leaning his head on my shoulder,
running his hand across my hips,
sharp rims of a broken clay bowl.
Our family is gnarled with branches,

anemic and leafless, specks of filtered sun,
bits of meals inhaled quickly, looking over one's
shoulder until not eating felt *released*
and air-pure. Is this another lesson
I'll lie awake in bed wondering if she'll turn

her stomach inside out to be rid of, then
swear she's not one of those girls
whose damaged, marked bodies rise up
through their throats?
I want to ask Jesus, already erased.

SIZE ZERO

Holding bread crust up to my lips,
I watch a crow hop past its black, feathered anchor
into *just a bit of atmosphere.*
My cat lunges into a rhododendron bush,

another January mouse pushed out of earth.
Disemboweled, its whiskered head will be left
behind like a misplaced chess piece
or bodiless, a perfect *size zero.*

My dog says it's time to eat again,
but she'll have to wait before dry food
hammers dinner into her blue bowl.
Outside, water thinly pours down the gutter,

drips just barely into a puddle.
Size zero—once, no weight or shape,
now these pants don't slip as easily
past my bones anymore.

How *did* I fill with them with zero,
slim-cut jeans carefully placed on the bed,
breath held, my body, a bluish flame
I perpetually gave birth to?

Released at the waist,
I never knew I could expand
like a choir, suddenly swelling
into a hallelujah,

my face glowing bright as a banjo.
I allow my body a few moments to settle.
In late morning's first splinters of light,
I allow it to stay.

STILL AS I WAS

1.

From the Magic 8-Ball passed
to our hands, ghostly white swirled
maybe every time we asked
if we were, in fact, the skinniest,
most flat-chested girls in Brunswick,
Ohio, filled with thorny cells
destined to die alone in our
beds with only our mothers there
to lean over us whispering
At least we're together now.

Our worried faces fall
through my memory
like confetti: who would inherit
our mother's long-stemmed black rose,
her dark caterpillar brows arched
above her eyes staring
deep into my blue as if asking:
*Where did you get them
and what do they mean?*

2.

I understand now it was his
illness talking, not mine,
the man I'd eventually leave
at the Mission Hill Green Line
stop, when he said if I ever
got sick whatever it was
would catch onto me like *fire
to a hay bale,* there was so little
of me to go around—why would he want
to marry me anyway? He had a list
of women's numbers locked
in a blue plastic bin in his closet.

But after a short week apart
he said what he had to offer
was too long, well-shaped,
too good to waste, I was the kind
of girl who looked good
naked in a wheat field,
a piece of oat nut bread
at my lips, yes, while I was still
young, he could imagine
me lying there on the white blanket
stroking his dog.

3.

I've survived waking
those first three months
to rainfall behind lace curtains,
my vein's tiny red puncture
like a jewel tucked into my arm
bent and resting across my chest.
I thought *sad* could be like
perfume lightly dabbed to my wrist,
not the granite rock holding
me prisoner all day in my bed,
lifted at night only by my rosary
that held up to lamplight
would glow pale green
draped around my opened fingers,
feeling every inch of my skin,
every rib, every mole,
wondering what, if anything,
has started its life in some secret

place I'll never know I even had
until the doctors tell me
It has to come out.
I've endured my husband's face,
pulled tight as a drum
skin by fear, his hands
flowing down my exposed back,
uncertain currents, words

spilling over and over
It makes no difference.
Nothing has changed.

4.

Still, every morning I pause
under white clouds swirling
across dense blue skies, a spare
canopy of black tree branches
destined to snap under the weight
of winter's first storm
but for now reach across
the road as if toward one another—
one past sagging telephone wires,
the other above brown
fouled underbrush,
a scattering of someone's
smashed Styrofoam cup,
coffee bled into mud.

The dark hollows of my eyes
are no longer those of a child
whose love for words
was stronger than her desire
to eat, hiding meat among
the sour cream, *the quiet one*
who held the bread
under her tongue
until she could roll it
like a wet damaged
bird onto a cloth.

5.

In the woods, slick toadstools
nudge their bald heads
through the damp earth,
poisonous in daylight,
tapped at night by more rain.
If I could roll my right shoulder

out of sleep, the side of my body
that cries to heal,

I could push the dirt
out of my mouth,
lift myself out of this animal
weight, call each morning

with a warble,
dawn turned to dust,
slight taste of blood, anemic lip.

6.

Night fields ripple so deeply
they disappear.
My eyes open to a black sky,
a slow rowing of moonlight,
the oarsman wearing
a cap dusted with Ohio wind.
It could be my father.
I don't answer the words
he calls to me,
his pale hand extended,
nails buffed into mirrors.

In my dream, my mother
tosses her walker
across the nursing home
dining room,
rushes back to him
holding her wrist up
see the bracelet
my daughter
got for me—
milky plastic rivulet,
each letter of her name
slowly rising.

7.

After four, not quite
five years, we welcome the new
scents my body gives off.
We name them
Sugar Pearl,
Black Lace Strap,
Red Feather from Above—

not Yankee Candle *Last Christmas You'll Ever See*
placed near the skin I was told
I might never feel again,
my right arm raised
over my head, resting
on the pillow.

Our mouths seal
to one another's breath.
We're done with spoken words.
Questions drop
onto the floor, answers
undress more slowly, stop,
unbuttoned, at the waist.

My Acupuncturist
Discovers a Point

where *good woman* meets *bad man.*
It burns like a hot cinder, makes me jump,
despite the lavender-scented satin pillow
stuffed and puffed into a diapered
moon cradling my face.
Have you been married before?

I could lie, facedown, staring through the hole
in the table and onto his seven-grain beige
carpeted floor. But he's onto something
touching my shoulder blades,
something the color of my tongue,
a deep *un-red* with a lightning-fire tear
down the middle, won't name.

From a table a dusty cloud
of moxa twists upward
past a brass bell. It smells heavily
of cigarettes, seeps into my coat
neatly placed on the chair.
Next to the bell, a carefully arranged
line of carved wooden elephants
labor toward us, trunks curled up for good luck.
Thirty years in practice, he's heard
many women complain

of constantly feeling cold,
felt their sluggish pulse
and not just in their hands or feet.
I could tell him how my first husband and I met,
shyly sharing a pole on the subway,
how years later, I learned to use prayer
like balm, slathered forgiveness

on the dog leash burning my legs,
the hand raised to my face, my neck
exposed, barely enough heft
in my voice to call the body back.
He rubs oil down my spine.
Your lungs are burdened
by the way you stand,

the way you sit—
Rising up from the table,
my blood rushes to the floor.
Six weeks, six sessions—
Could be, he says lightly
patting my back,
you just don't like the cold.

THE FOX

At night I hear it screaming as if it's being robbed.
There are signs of other wildlife too.
It must be that I'm dreaming—headlights, a car coming to a stop.

Who unlocked the gate?
A deer stands motionless—lost, but in view.
At night I hear screaming. Is someone being robbed?

Coyotes break from a shadowed mob,
Raccoons, opossums, wafting pool of skunk.
It could be that I'm dreaming, the sound of a car stopped.

Whose flashlights unearth each barren den?
Daylight witnesses are too few.
At night I hear it screaming, as if someone's being robbed.

I lived so long without it—
Fire streak, a flick of russet tail. Perhaps I was only
Dreaming, no blood trail found or stopped.

How brief the wilderness at last had come.
Awakened, it wouldn't stay.
At night I hear it screaming, as if being robbed.
It must be that I'm sleeping, the sound of dreaming stopped.

TO SEE A HORSE

. . . in human flesh, descending on a hammock through the
air, and as it nears your house is metamorphosed into a
man, and he approaches your door and throws something
at you which seems to be rubber but turns into great bees,
denotes miscarriage of hopes and useless endeavors . . .
　　　　　—The Dictionary of Dreams,
　　　　　　Gustavas Hindman Miller

Its forelock she'd mistaken
　　　for a flaring match
　　　　　then rising from a hayfield

his shape eclipsing the sun
　　　shovel in his hand She'd
　　　　　released a swarm of bees

each time she opened
　　　her mouth certain
　　　　　they were words

Night after night
　　　he strikes her in the face
　　　　　but she will not leave him

thick netting settling
　　　across her lap
　　　　　He strikes her legs

She will not complain about him
　　　No frustrations or loss of hope
　　　　　as long as the shovel doesn't break

Awake now in her family's basement
　　　she gently rubs his honey bathrobe
　　　　　against her face

light smell of shower
        water soap
                She only remembers circles of snow

blowing upward as if retreating
        to sky his slow
                walking toward her

now standing on the rug
        where underneath he'd scarred
                with a pocketknife their names

the wood given in to promise
        how that night he called her *mouse*
                my mouse of all things

and she said yes

MUSE

He even tried it once—throwing his legs over his head in a kind
of weird yoga tree pose, doing his best to enact going down on
himself. I, impressed, thanked him for telling me something
so cutting edge, for having the balls to be so honest. There's
more, he said, moving closer to me on the porch swing. He'd
been considering cutting a hole in melon and, right there in the
park, getting *real personal* with it . . . —as a joke, just to blow
the minds of the town's college professors and interdisciplinary
majors away—something about performance-body-art. I listened
carefully, my legs folded under me, naked under my loose Batik
dress, an orchid tucked behind my ear, never thinking by the end
of August I'd lie in a sunlit grass field for him, summer humming
hungry and open around us. I'd be his muse. I never thought
he'd leave me for the blond one-car-garage-band guitarist who'd
leave him for a short-tempered water-colorist, never thinking,
twenty years later, at the dinner table, turning my head from
my husband, quietly spitting watermelon seeds into my cupped
hand, black and slippery, one sticking to my lip, I'd want so
badly to phone him, hear him try to guess who it was on the
other end of the line—me, the muse he swore on his life he'd
never forget—feel his whole body straining into his tongue's tip,
coming up just a few inches short.

STUNG

Barbed wire fences
keep score,
each knot a hitch
on thorn rope—

petal-less rose
grasping its steely life,
guitar string just before
snapped broken,

last note flung into air.

NORTH OF PATSY CLINE
—for H-B

My daughter presses a mini recorder
like a conch shell up to my ear

and whispers *Listen.*
It is her fifteen-year-old voice

singing about heartache—
mommas and daddies crying, cursing the wind,

swearing never to love again.
But we are still safe, years north of that day

when our hearts fall,
when even my lit silk orchid branches

reaching up from the floor can't lift us,
when we won't quite clear

the treetops, but hit instead on rocky ground
with Hawkins, Copas and Hughes,

into the swamp of Cline
some five jagged miles off the Tennessee River—

Poland Spring bottles
hidden at the bottom of a crowded gym bag, one bottle

at a time, not a lick of water
in that well-kept, long running, secret well.

PROLONGED

Promise me heavy wagons, trodden grasses,
smoke rising from deep within woods,
the open pit fire.

Promise me hunger and a voice with which to answer
the *never was* dinner bell.

Promise me a room that drinks in night,
chairs and beds that never existed
and therefore can't be moved.

Promise me
the wick that burns with words that refuse to leave
its prolonged sentence,

Thursdays, starless and idle
that surprise us with Friday's green, furrowed paths.

Promise me the alarm clock that misplaces its hatchet,
the prescribed pill that gets over itself,

the mailed letter capable of crying.
Anything unfolded can cry.

Promise me midnight's passing winter rain—
street lamp, moon lamp

on the other side.

MEMORIZING MUSIC

Leave desire unmeasured; let your body unfold
toward an unmarked pitch. If your eyes
tighten, you're thinking too hard.
Feel instead yourself reaching
past winter's black keys,
toward the page-turner who loves each last note
that makes her rise.

But if you must count out triplets
with a metronome and in rhymes
remember *beau-ti-ful e-ven-ing*
as the last of a summer storm,
a swamp singing through soft bodies,
damp, hollowed seeds on the circular shore.

EARLY HOUR

The moon would rather be a rock star.
So it hangs onto the night sky, spot light and open door.
For the man and woman tired of its one tune,
it offers a burning candle's trail of smoke
that rises and goes nowhere,
a piece of bed gliding through an MRI.
It says sleep is for woodpeckers tired of drumming,
for a family of deer who have leapt into a pond of ferns.
Instead, the moon urges *live*.
The black leather jacket drops into words about a black leather jacket.
The crimson firefly swells at the tip of a cigarette.
And you know it, standing alone in your yard,
closing your book of poems by Yevtushenko,
that this is the grand reunion tour—
the constant hammering in your brain
naked mind, naked body—in daylight
butterflies that will die if they hitchhike onto your clothes.

Notes

The ending line in "Black Dog" *that we have come* is inspired by James Wright's "A Blessing": *they can hardly contain their happiness / That we have come.* This poem was written for Solstice Director, Meg Kearney.

"Borscht" was written for Jeff Friedman.

"Stolen" was written for my sister, Maria Sestina.

In "Firing My Father's Mossberg," the couplet, *And spirited from sleep, the astounded soul / Hangs for a moment bodiless and simple* is taken from Richard Wilbur's poem "Love Calls Us to the Things of This World."

"Memorizing Music" is for Eugene Kaminsky. Thank you, in particular, for Saint-Saëns.

"Prolonged" was written for Franz Wright.

"The crimson firefly swells at the tip of a cigarette" in "Early Hour" is a variation of the line "the crimson firefly of a cigarette" translated by John Updike with Albert C. Todd in Yevgeny Yevtushenko's poem "New York Elegy." This poem was written for Ray González, and John Martyn.

Some previous titles in the Carnegie Mellon Poetry Series

2010
The Diminishing House, Nicky Beer
A World Remembered, T. Alan Broughton
Say Sand, Daniel Coudriet
Knock Knock, Heather Hartley
In the Land We Imagined Ourselves, Jonathan Johnson
Selected Early Poems: 1958-1983, Greg Kuzma
The Other Life: Selected Poems, Herbert Scott
Admission, Jerry Williams

2009
Divine Margins, Peter Cooley
Cultural Studies, Kevin A. González
Dear Apocalypse, K. A. Hays
Warhol-o-rama, Peter Oresick
Cave of the Yellow Volkswagen, Maureen Seaton
Group Portrait from Hell, David Schloss
Birdwatching in Wartime, Jeffrey Thomson

2008
The Grace of Necessity, Samuel Green
After West, James Harms
Anticipate the Coming Reservoir, John Hoppenthaler
Convertible Night, Flurry of Stones, Dzvinia Orlowsky
Parable Hunter, Ricardo Pau-Llosa
The Book of Sleep, Eleanor Stanford

2007
Trick Pear, Suzanne Cleary
So I Will Till the Ground, Gregory Djanikian
Black Threads, Jeff Friedman
Drift and Pulse, Kathleen Halme
The Playhouse Near Dark, Elizabeth Holmes
On the Vanishing of Large Creatures, Susan Hutton

One Season Behind, Sarah Rosenblatt
Indeed I Was Pleased with the World, Mary Ruefle
The Situation, John Skoyles

2006
Burn the Field, Amy Beeder
The Sadness of Others, Hayan Charara
A Grammar to Waking, Nancy Eimers
Dog Star Delicatessen: New and Selected Poems 1979–2006, Mekeel McBride
Shinemaster, Michael McFee
Eastern Mountain Time, Joyce Peseroff
Dragging the Lake, Robert Thomas

2005
Things I Can't Tell You, Michael Dennis Browne
Bent to the Earth, Blas Manuel De Luna
Blindsight, Carol Hamilton
Fallen from a Chariot, Kevin Prufer
Needlegrass, Dennis Sampson
Laws of My Nature, Margot Schilpp
Sleeping Woman, Herbert Scott
Renovation, Jeffrey Thomson

2004
The Women Who Loved Elvis All Their Lives, Fleda Brown
The Chronic Liar Buys a Canary, Elizabeth Edwards
Freeways and Aqueducts, James Harms
Prague Winter, Richard Katrovas
Trains in Winter, Jay Meek
Tristimania, Mary Ruefle
Venus Examines Her Breast, Maureen Seaton
Various Orbits, Thom Ward

2000
Blue Jesus, Jim Daniels
Years Later, Gregory Djanikian
Winter Morning Walks: 100 Postcards to Jim Harrison, Ted Kooser
Mortal Education, Joyce Peseroff
How Things Are, James Richardson
On the Waterbed They Sank to Their Own Levels, Sarah Rosenblatt
Post Meridian, Mary Ruefle
Constant Longing, Dennis Sampson
Hierarchies of Rue, Roger Sauls
Small Boat with Oars of Different Size, Thom Ward